Alberto Moravia

by
LUCIANO REBAY

 **Columbia University Press**
NEW YORK & LONDON 1970

COLUMBIA ESSAYS ON MODERN WRITERS
is a series of critical studies of English, Continental, and other writers whose works are of contemporary artistic and intellectual significance.

Editor

William York Tindall

Advisory Editors

Jacques Barzun   W. T. H. Jackson   Joseph A. Mazzeo

Alberto Moravia is Number 52 of the series

LUCIANO REBAY
is Professor of Italian at Columbia University.
He is the author of *Le origini della poesia di Giuseppe Ungaretti* and *Invitation to Italian Poetry*.

Copyright © 1970 Columbia University Press
ISBN: 0-231-02762-1
Library of Congress Catalog Card Number: 77-126544
Printed in the United States of America

Acknowledgment is made to Farrar, Straus & Giroux, Inc., for permission to quote extracts from the following titles by Alberto Moravia: from *The Woman of Rome*, copyright 1949 by Valentino Bompiani & Co., S.A.; from *The Time of Indifference*, copyright 1953 by Valentino Bompiani & Co.; from *The Empty Canvas*, copyright © 1961 by Valentino Bompiani & Co.; from *The Lie*, copyright © 1966 by Casa Ed. Valentino Bompiani.

Alberto Moravia

The best introduction to the work of Alberto Moravia has been provided by the author himself. In an autobiographical essay (1958) he remarks:

The dominant theme of my work appears to be man's relationship with reality. Although to some this may seem a strictly philosophical problem, it is the fundamental issue of our time. It reached its most acute stage during and immediately after World War I because of the war's total destruction of the traditional scale of values; a destruction which brought about a sudden interruption and complete collapse of that relationship between man and reality which until then had been based on traditional ethics. Without warning man found himself incapable of establishing any relationship whatsoever with his own world, which thereafter appeared to him obscure and indecipherable—or worse still, nonexistent. My first novel, *The Time of Indifference*, and the others that followed have tried to express through realistic characters and situations the urgency of this crisis.

This is actually more than an introduction, for the passage is filled with implications that can be appreciated only as one reads Moravia's novels and short stories, especially in their order of publication. That his writings express a tragic sense of emptiness becomes apparent rather quickly, but the fact in itself does not signify enough until one sees it as the consequence of twentieth-century man's inability to relate to reality —both to his own and to that of his time. One may even conclude that the central theme of Moravia's fiction is—to use a phrase made famous by Paul Valéry—"the crisis of the spirit." This crisis involves all aspects of Moravia's production; it is, for example (again in his own words), "responsible for the role that sex plays" in his writings, "sex being one of the most primitive and unchanging modes of rapport with reality."

Any "explanation" of this kind is double-edged—and, to be sure, some adverse critics have used the passage to disparage its author's achievement. For instance, Moravia has been accused, by some, of producing pornography; by others, of being a "monotonous" writer who has written all told but "one book." Despite Moravia's own clarification of the role played by sex in his work, all his books were placed on the Index in 1952. As for the second charge—of being "monotonous"—he gladly accepts it. Most artists, he points out, have only a limited number of things to say and, just as birds repeat the same songs, artists repeat the same themes, varying the tone, however, from year to year.

Alberto Pincherle Moravia was born in Rome on November 28, 1907. The commonly held belief that "Moravia" is a pseudonym has no foundation in fact; nevertheless, a number of serious critics have attributed to him the authorship of a book of poems, *Diciotto liriche in memoria di Bianca Pesenti* (Eighteen Lyrics in Memory of Bianca Pesenti), by one Alberto Pincherle, even though it was published in Rome in 1920 when Moravia was thirteen years old. When I inquired about this alleged "opus primum," Moravia dismissed the whole matter with an ironic smile. True, he said, he had written many poems—"bad" poems—up to the age of sixteen, but they were never published and they have now disappeared. As for the 1920 book, its author, it turns out, is now a university professor of religion by the name of Alberto Pincherle, and, so far as Moravia knows, not a relative. He termed the attribution of the volume in question to a thirteen-year-old child as "monstrous." Pincherle, he said, had been his family's name until the early nineteenth century, at which time he believes his great-grandfather added the name Moravia as a tribute to a Triestine friend who had left him an inheritance. (Alberto Moravia has not used his middle name since 1928 precisely to avoid confusion with Alberto Pincherle.)

Moravia's father, an architect, was a Venetian Jew. His mother, née De Marsanich, is a countess of Dalmatian origin, and a Catholic. Moravia, like his brother and two sisters, was baptized and reared as a Catholic. His religious upbringing, however, was superficial and formal. "Religion never played an important role in our home," he declared during a recent discussion. "My father was an atheist who had no interest in Judaism and never went to the synagogue. My mother was a practicing Catholic only insofar as she went to mass on Sunday. However, just before my father's death in 1944, she had him baptized so that he would die a Christian!" Personally, Moravia never had any real rapport with his father, a solitary, timid, yet choleric man who seldom spoke to his children. He was somewhat closer to his mother, whom he describes as an extremely simple woman, with little education. What concerned her was not so much culture or religion but being accepted by the bourgeois society of Rome. "In short," Moravia concludes, "we were a very conventional family. My parents had an automobile with chauffeur and a box at the Opera, but they seemed to do all these things out of some mechanical necessity. As for me, the Roman society with which they were trying to mingle appeared simply horrible, even before I could understand the reasons for my revulsion."

At the age of nine Moravia was stricken with a serious case of tuberculosis of the leg bone, and for the next nine years he was constantly ill, save for brief intervals of temporary improvement. As a consequence he had to abandon his formal studies and was unable to graduate from high school. Instead, he spent the long years of his enforced idleness reading every book he could find, in Italian or French, and later in English and German as well. His mother, who was planning to have him enter the diplomatic service, had engaged a succession of foreign governesses so that he could learn their respective languages. So it was that he came to speak French fluently even before Italian and to experience literature first in French, through the novels of Madame de Ségur. As he grew older he began to use his father's library, which was particularly rich in theatre classics—Goldoni, Molière, Racine, Shakespeare. Finally, having become a member of the largest private circulating library in Italy, the Biblioteca Vieusseux of Florence, he embarked on a regime of reading an average of one book every two days. He would concentrate on a single author at a time, and thanks to this systematic "method," he became familiar with the works of such writers as Dostoevsky, Joyce, Baudelaire, Rimbaud, Stendhal, Flaubert, Proust, Balzac, De Maupassant, Boccaccio, Manzoni, Verga, and Pirandello.

His illness had forced Moravia to spend five years in bed: three at home in Rome, and the last two, from 1923 to 1925, in the sanatorium Codivilla at Cortina d'Ampezzo in the Dolomites. Those last two years, the most critical for his health, were important psychologically and emotionally as well, for they emancipated him at last from his family. Moravia makes no mystery today of the fact that he was unhappy living at home, bored with the household routine, and that he holds a totally negative view of the family as an institution within the bourgeois social structure. "The most mistaken teachings," he said in a scathing declaration published on December 29, 1965, in Milan's conservative newspaper *Corriere della sera*, "are those given by the family. The Italian family, moreover, is in most cases a temple for the worship of such divinities as Prudence, Self-interest, Ignorance, Hedonism. . . . Any school at all, even the worst, is better than the family." One cannot fail to note in this connection that Moravia's first novel, *The Time of Indifference*, is a pitiless story of the moral disintegration of an upper middle-class Roman family devoted to those very "divinities."

This coincidence—if the word applies—raises the question of "autobiography," in relation not only to Moravia's first book but to his entire production. Again, he himself provides the answer in straightforward terms. "My novels are usually based on a particular experience of my life, an experience which I try of course to filter, to analyze in depth. A writer's work is always 'autobiographical,' obviously, for one can talk only of what one has known or experienced. Michele, the protagonist of *The Time of Indifference*, is clearly a projection of myself. The persona of this lonesome and unhappy boy already existed in my mind when I was eleven years old, which is to say that the novel grew out of many years of incubation. On the other hand, plot, characters, and individual situations of this and other novels are not necessarily factually true; they are indeed almost always invented, and in this sense I say that my work is not autobiographical." Moravia remembers having started to write very early in life, when he was eight or nine, and continuing until he was sixteen, the year he entered the sanatorium. For the ensuing two years he was allowed no activity except reading, but at eighteen, when he was discharged, he took up writing again and in the space of five years, from 1925 to 1930, produced three short stories and a novel. These works, which remain among his best, portray a world disintegrating, a society of individuals trapped in a circle of indifference, cynicism, cruelty, and boredom.

Of the three short stories, two—"Cortigiana stanca" (Tired Courtesan) and "Delitto al circolo di tennis" (Crime at the Tennis Club)—were written while Moravia was also working on *The Time of Indifference;* and in several respects they anticipate this first novel. "Cortigiana stanca" appeared in 1927 in the avant-garde review *900,* which was published in Italy by Italians but entirely in French. This story, Moravia's first printed work, did not come out in the Italian original until 1935, when it formed part of a volume ironically entitled *La bella vita* (The Beautiful Life). "Cortigiana stanca" is a rather romantic description of the decline of a once beautiful demimondaine, Maria Teresa, whose lovers had showered her with money and attention when she was young. Now, on the threshold of old age, unattractive and penniless, she turns for help to her first protector. He is very rich, but refuses even to see her. In sharp contrast to her pathetic situation we see, on the one hand, the disdainful indifference of this older man and, on the other, the cutting cynicism of her latest lover, a young man who has kept her for two months and now coldly plans to abandon her. As he walks to her house for what he has decided will be their last meeting, he keeps imagining "with a sort of furious will a Maria Teresa laden with years, her breasts hanging down, her fat belly trembling above the slackened joints of her groin, her hips pasty and shapeless—in short, a Maria Teresa on the verge of old age, whom it would be a pleasure to abandon."

"To the devil with Maria Teresa!" is the young man's last thought when a few hours later he leaves her—an attitude re-echoed in the opening pages of the novel *The Time of Indifference.* Leo Merumeci, an unscrupulous businessman, bored with his fifteen-year relationship with Mariagrazia, attempts to persuade her daughter, Carla, to become his mistress: "Break away

—he repeated—Come and live with me. . . . We'll part company with your mother and send her to the devil. . . . She can go to hell. . . ." Yet even closer affinities to the particular atmosphere of *The Time of Indifference* may be seen in the second story, "Crime at the Tennis Club," also written in 1927. Here we are introduced to the problem of "boredom," a recurrent theme not only in Moravia's first novel but in much of his later work as well (one of his most significant novels is entitled *La noia* [Boredom]).

"Crime at the Tennis Club," like "Tired Courtesan," is a fast-moving story. Its style, somewhat reminiscent of Hemingway, whom Moravia admired, is rapid and precise. Free of wasted words and lengthy, drawn-out descriptions, it reveals a deftness and a formal control which are truly remarkable in an author barely twenty years old. The plot is simple, dramatic. The members of a well-known tennis club, all of them offspring of rich and respected upper middle-class families, decide to give a gala ball and to include the "Princess" among the guests. The "Princess" is in fact a countess who, though no longer young or beautiful, is still vain and eager for masculine company. She is also known to be very fond of liquor, and the intention of the tennis club members in inviting her is to provide free entertainment for the party by getting her drunk. But what was first conceived as a callous joke unexpectedly turns into a crime. One of the group, Ripandelli, after plying the woman with drink and flattering her vanity with feigned gallantry, becomes enraged at her desperate resistance when he and some others try to undress her. He strikes her on the head with a bottle, killing her instantly. Once the first moment of shock and consternation has passed, the young assassin and his friends turn to the problem of disposing of the body. Very coldly and matter-of-factly a certain Jancovich, the oldest of the group, suggests throwing the "Princess" into the river. "It will be thought that she killed herself in a moment of depression," he says. "We will rejoin the other guests in the ballroom and behave as if nothing had happened." And so it is done.

Basically the characters of this chilling story belong to the same human cast that composes *The Time of Indifference:* members of a corrupt society which has lost all sense of proportion and purpose, individuals who drift through life unable to resist the attraction of even the most degrading experiences in an attempt to find an escape from the immense boredom that afflicts them. For Italian readers the theme of boredom automatically suggests the name of Giacomo Leopardi. But the romantic ennui of that great nineteenth-century poet is a cosmic feeling of an essentially philosophical and intellectual nature which finds, as it were, theoretical expression in reflection and thought. In practice, while lamenting the vanity of life and deprecating man's destined unhappiness, Leopardi accepts, or rather endures, things as they are, ennui included.

The boredom of Moravia's characters is of a later origin; its sources lie in that crucible of "decadent" romantic literature which is Baudelaire's *Les fleurs du mal*. Baudelaire, long one of Moravia's favorite authors, defines ennui in the opening lines of his masterwork as the ugliest, filthiest, most evil monster in the infamous menagerie of human vices; and in the closing poem of the book, after referring to man's existence as an oasis of horror in a desert of boredom, he begs death to pour him its poison, for he wants to "plunge to the bottom of the abyss," of the unknown, be it hell or paradise, in order to find something "NEW" ("du NOUVEAU"). Boredom thus becomes a source of man's will to change, a spur to action—any action that might break the vicious circle started by boredom itself and reestablish the lost link with reality. Baudelaire's image of "plunging to the bottom of the abyss" describes with literal exactness, as Moravia himself readily acknowledges, the behavior of some of his most typical characters, beginning with the two protagonists of his first novel, *The Time of Indifference.*

This book, whose Italian title is *Gli indifferenti* (literally, "The Indifferent Ones"), is the detailed account of what happens to the members of a Roman family, the Ardengos, and to two of their friends in the course of forty-eight hours. The general structure is thus distantly reminiscent of Joyce's *Ulysses,* which Moravia started reading soon after leaving the sanatorium. He points out, however, that what prompted him to limit the narrative to a very brief time-span was chiefly his desire to write a novel that would have some of the characteristics of a play and would respect as much as possible the Aristotelian unities of time, place, and action. He did not want, he says, so much to "narrate," as to "represent." *The Time of Indifference* is, in other words, a dramatic fiction. It was composed as an "oral" work, with only dashes marking the pauses in the text. Formal punctuation was added to the final manuscript at the insistence of the publisher. The dramatis personae are Mariagrazia Ardengo, a middle-aged widow who deludes herself into believing she is still young and attractive; her children Carla and Michele; Leo Merumeci, a real estate dealer, who, as mentioned above, has been Mariagrazia's lover for fifteen years; and Lisa, Leo's former mistress and fiancée, now the principal cause of Mariagrazia's recurrent scenes of jealousy. Mariagrazia does not know that her present rival is her own daughter, Carla, and that Lisa is trying to woo Michele, not Leo.

The novel opens with Leo's attempt to seduce Carla. The man is a frequent visitor at the Ardengo residence, not only because of his liaison with Mariagrazia, but also as a result of his business dealings with her. Having gained control of the Ardengos' financial future, he is about to acquire possession of their house, an expensive villa on which he holds the mortgage. Leo's abrupt proposal to Carla to become his mistress finds the young girl unexpectedly acquiescent. Not that Carla has any illusions about her feelings for Leo: she does not love him. But she is also unwilling to tolerate any longer the falsity and boredom of life in her mother's house. Carla is aware that her chances of marrying a respectable man have been reduced to almost nil by Mariagrazia's disreputable affair with Leo. Having lost respect for herself, she has reached a point where all she cares about is changing her existence, as soon as possible, no matter how, and at any price:

Again she made the futile gesture of trying to push Leo away from her, but more feebly than before, for now a kind of resignation had taken possession of her: why should she refuse Leo? Virtue would merely throw her back into the arms of boredom and the distasteful trivialities of everyday habit; and it seemed to her, furthermore, that this present adventure, with its air of familiarity, was the only epilogue her old life deserved; afterwards, everything would be new—both life and herself. She looked at the man's face, close to her, held out towards her. "End it all," she thought, "ruin everything." And her brain whirled as though she were about to hurl herself foremost into space.

Later on, exasperated by yet another outburst of Mariagrazia's jealously, Carla decides that on the following day, her twenty-fourth birthday, she will give herself to Leo, thus becoming the mistress of her mother's lover:

Even this ignoble coincidence, this rivalry with her mother, pleased her; everything must be impure, dirty, low, there must be neither love nor affection, but only a dark sense of ruin. "I must create a scandalous, impossible situation, full of scenes and hopelessly shameful," she said to herself, "I must ruin myself utterly."

The evening of her birthday, she slips out of the house and

spends the night in Leo's apartment. She returns there the following afternoon, but this time the tryst is interrupted by the arrival of Michele.

A few years younger than Carla, Michele is the novel's pivotal and most complex character. His seemingly total, invincible indifference to everything and everybody is reflected in the title, *Gli indifferenti*. But there is also in Michele "an unbearable disgust at his own versatile indifference which allowed him to change his ideas and attitudes every day as other people change their clothes." The young man yearns to be different—a tragic, sincere, instinctive person capable of faith, of respect and love for his mother, and of hate for Leo. He especially longs to find "among all the people in the world, a woman whom he could love sincerely, without irony and without resignation." It is all wishful thinking, however: each time the opportunity for action presents itself, he invariably feels "inert, leaden; there was no inkling of anger, or rage, or hatred . . . —nothing had the power to shake him. . . . For him, faith, sincerity, a sense of the tragic, no longer existed; everything, seen through the veil of his boredom, appeared pitiful, ridiculous, artificial." Nevertheless, the obsession to act, to conquer his indifference, continues to pursue him, giving him no peace.

The unexpected revelation that Carla has been seduced by Leo seems at last to offer him the occasion for a dramatic, spectacular deed. It is Lisa, whose advances Michele has rejected, who informs him out of spite that she has seen Carla and Leo embracing. Even this news fails at first to shake Michele. But then he decides in desperation that the time has come for him "to make up his mind, once and for all, to make a pretence of *everything*—of love, of hatred, of indignation—a pretence on a big scale, in the grand manner." He therefore decides to kill Leo. But he forgets to load his revolver; as he repeatedly squeezes the trigger, it is as though his overwhelming indifference had affected even his weapon. While Leo easily disarms his assailant, Carla, half-dressed, comes in from the bedroom. Michele beseeches her to give up her lover, promising that the two of them will begin a new life, will sell the villa and pay Leo. The sale of the villa on the free market, however, would prevent Leo from making a very large profit, and he proposes a different solution, much less heroic and honorable than Michele's but more practical and socially acceptable. He will marry Carla, help Michele find a good job; he will even consent to have Mariagrazia live with them. Carla does not have the strength to turn down such a settlement; nor for that matter does Michele, when his sister announces that she is ready to marry Leo. Although Moravia does not say so explicitly, the concluding pages of the novel leave little doubt concerning Michele's fate: he will passively accept both Leo's protection and Lisa's love and continue to flow with the current of events and social conventions without feelings or will of his own.

The Time of Indifference was issued in Milan in July, 1929, by Alpes, a little-known publishing house, and at the author's expense. The manuscript had been refused by all the major publishers. Its appearance created a sensation; in a few months the novel had five successive printings and sold 5000 copies, a very sizable number at a time when 700 or 800 was considered a mark of success. One of the most influential writers and critics of those years, Giuseppe Antonio Borgese, hailed Moravia's "creative genius." His enthusiasm, however, was by no means shared by all, particularly not by the Fascist press. Although the Fascist regime at that time was still relatively liberal, or perhaps uninterested in cultural matters, it could not ignore for long a book which painted such an unflattering picture of

Italian society, and specifically of Italian youth. Mussolini's brother Arnaldo stated in a public speech that he was opposed to having young Italians read an author such as Moravia, "a destroyer of every human value." Soon afterwards the publisher was advised to cease distributing the book.

In retrospect there seems no doubt that this first novel remains one of Moravia's most impressive achievements; some regard it as his very best. Apart from its purely literary qualities —its verbal freshness and aggressiveness, its almost clinical style, bare of external embellishment—*The Time of Indifference* holds a place of prominence in the history of twentieth-century fiction. Preceding by nine years Sartre's *La Nausée* (Nausea) and by thirteen Camus's *L'Etranger* (The Stranger), it is a forerunner of the existentialist novel, as the late Jean Paulhan, director of *La Nouvelle Revue Française*, acutely noted in 1948 during one of Moravia's visits to Paris. Moravia, on his part, rejects the definition of existentialist in strictly philosophical terms. His existentialism, he says, was in no way dogmatic; it was simply dictated by his painful awareness of man's difficulty in establishing a satisfactory rapport with reality. When he wrote *The Time of Indifference*, he assures us, he was not familiar with the writings of Heidegger or Jaspers. By the same token he had not read either Freud or Marx, with whose works he became superficially acquainted only years later. The father of modern fiction—hence of literary existentialism—is, in his opinion, Dostoevsky. And it is to the Russian master, on the one side, and to French nineteenth-century "decadent" writers, on the other, that he personally feels most indebted. Michele's problem in *The Time of Indifference* is the relationship between man and action, and this is a problem that takes us back to *The Brothers Karamazov*, to *The Obsessed*, and of course to Raskolnikov in *Crime and Punishment*.

To the same general climate of what Moravia calls "Dostoevskian existentialism" belongs a haunting short story he wrote one year after the publication of *The Time of Indifference,* "Inverno di malato" (A Patient's Winter). Again we experience the depressing atmosphere of boredom that hangs over the existence of the tennis club members, and of Carla, Mariagrazia, and Leo. Here too boredom inevitably leads to the "abyss." The protagonist of the story is Girolamo, a boy suffering from tuberculosis of the knee bone. A patient at a sanatorium in the mountains (the setting recalls the Codivilla clinic), he shares a room with a traveling salesman, a certain Brambilla, an older, crude, vulgar man. To kill the monotony of the interminable hours, Brambilla amuses himself by heaping scorn on Girolamo, whom he derides particularly for his sexual inexperience. In order to win Brambilla's respect and to stop the relentless teasing, Girolamo one day decides to seduce a fourteen-year-old English girl into whose room he is often wheeled to keep her company. Despite the strong revulsion he feels at his own plan, he tries to make love to her—but without success. His visits are stopped after the girl, in a delirium, tells her doctor about the attempted seduction. Brambilla, cured, soon leaves the sanatorium. Girolamo finds himself again utterly alone, ashamed, frustrated, despairing even that he will ever recover from his illness.

Dostoevsky's impact continued, according to Moravia's own admission, for at least six years after *The Time of Indifference,* a period during which he painstakingly wrote his second novel, *Le ambizioni sbagliate* (literally, "Wrong Ambitions," translated into English first as *The Wheel of Fortune,* then as *Mistaken Ambitions*). But the deliberate attempt to compose a "Dostoevskian novel"—a vast, panoramic, eighteenth-century-like fresco of the Italian bourgeoisie under Fascism, with numerous characters and an intricate plot—resulted in failure. Moravia is the first to acknowledge humorously that writing *Le ambizioni sbagliate* was probably a "wrong ambition." With typical candor he confesses that after completing *The Time of Indifference* he felt he had exhausted all that he had or wished to say. On the other hand, he wanted to continue working, and so he started a new novel which he wrote and rewrote compulsively until he published it in 1935. In compliance with instructions sent by the government to all newspapers and literary journals expressly forbidding any mention of it, the book received no critical response, not even one review.

Le ambizioni sbagliate is Moravia's longest book, almost 500 pages of small print. The title derives from the fact that ambition, which the author singles out as perhaps the most destructive aspect of human egoism, is the passion that dominates every activity of the characters in the story. These are no longer, like Michele and Carla, apathetic and indifferent, but avid, aggressive, cruel, and vengeful. Yet, encumbered as it is by too many characters and plot entanglements, the novel lacks the sharpness of focus of *The Time of Indifference*. While agreeing that *Le ambizioni sbagliate* was not successful, indeed while stating flatly that he does not like it, Moravia points out that this book was useful to him insofar as it clarified his own limitations. "It freed me from the obsession of trying to identify with and follow the different viewpoints of different characters," he states. "And it convinced me that, for me at least, the best approach to fiction in our century was that of *The Time of Indifference:* very few characters and a fairly simple plot. I therefore decided that henceforth I would adopt the viewpoint of only one character." In his subsequent works he abided by this resolution.

After *Le ambizioni sbagliate* Moravia did not find again the vein of the long novel for more than ten years. During this period he produced dozens of short stories and two short novels, while at the same time traveling extensively—he was a guest for several months at Columbia University's Casa Italiana; he went to Mexico, England, France, China, and Greece. Among the most interesting short stories are those of a satirical and surrealistic inspiration, aimed more or less overtly at the social, cultural, and political situation in Italy under Mussolini. Two of the most typical are "In punto di morte" (At the Point of Death, 1940) and "L'epidemia" (The Epidemic, 1944). The first is a sarcastic, biting philippic against literary criticism and the devastating effects that can be wrought upon the literature of a country by a nationally revered pundit. One such man, the critic S., summons to his deathbed a close friend, a novelist, to make an extraordinary confession. His entire life, he declares, has been a lie. He had wanted to be a poet and had taken up criticism only after becoming convinced that he could never be creative. At the same time he had vowed out of revenge to ruin any writers endowed with genuine creative talent by using his influence to put them systematically on the wrong track: if they showed a gift for poetry he would persuade them to try the novel or playwriting, and vice versa. Not one contemporary author had escaped, says S., and as a result he was responsible for his country's being "deprived of a literature that could have been outstanding." After these words S. dies, leaving his friend completely baffled, for he himself had been encouraged by S. to be a novelist rather than a poet or an essayist. Meanwhile the name of the defunct critic is exalted in the best literary circles. His friend damns him in his heart, but decides to join the unanimous chorus of praise and to conceal the deathbed confession. The second story, "L'epidemia," is a savage caricature of a country whose inhabitants' heads, with few exceptions, suddenly start to smell as though in a state of putrefaction. As a result of the strange epidemic, most of the citizens gradually lose their olfactory sense or, more precisely, come to regard their own smell and all other smells as pleasant odors. The bitter allegory is unmistakable: Fascism, with its propaganda, corruption, and intimidation, had so debased the Italian people that they were no longer able to distinguish between good and evil.

Political satire is at the origin also of the first of the two short novels that Moravia wrote before the fall of Fascism, *La mascherata* (The Masquerade, 1941, translated into English as *The Fancy Dress Party*). "I had the almost physical need to write something against totalitarian dictatorships," he affirms, "but it was of course impossible to do it in a realistic exposé. The satire had to be presented in a kind of picturesque cellophane wrapping, transparent enough but capable at the same time of creating a festive appearance. I found the wrapping I was looking for during a trip to Mexico and wrote a folkloristic fable set against the background of a hypothetical South American state." *La mascherata*, however, lacks the light touch and the subtle irony and humor of Moravia's best satirical short stories. The plot, revolving around the lust and gallant conquests of a dictator, General Tereso, and thickly interwoven with a maze of amorous entanglements, assassination plans, murders, and imbroglios, is excessively baroque and makes for heavy reading. More interesting, though not from a literary but a sociopolitical point of view, is the novel's reception in Italy. No one at the Ministry for Popular Culture, not even the minister who had final responsibility for literary censorship, seemed to know what to do with such a work. In the uncertainty the decision was left to Mussolini personally. At first he permitted the book to be printed and distributed, then reversed himself and ordered it to be confiscated.

Of incomparably higher literary quality is the second short

novel, *Agostino*, whose publication was vetoed by the authorities in 1942. It came out two years later, in Rome, after the liberation of the city by the Allies. Moravia recalls having written the story in Capri, "in a few hours," and one senses in reading it that it is indeed the product of a strong, quasi-lyrical inspiration. The opening pages, which describe the serene, idyllic entente between the thirteen-year-old Agostino and his widowed mother before the arrival of her young suitor —the event that sets in motion Agostino's crisis of alienation and confidence—are possibly the most moving and stylistically brilliant in all Moravia's fiction. These pages are the more remarkable for being the work of a clear, lucid, analytical writer who is much more interested in "substance" than in stylistic effects per se. Moravia has never been, like a whole school of his contemporaries, a conscious practitioner or admirer of the so-called "prosa d'arte" ("art prose"). Indeed this fact goes far in explaining the disfavor in which he has always been held by a sizable portion of Italian critics—for the most part, the same critics who have reservations about such authors as Verga, Svevo, Pirandello, and Silone because in their opinion they do not write with sufficient "elegance." "I have never cultivated style in a mere formalistic sense, as a verbal exercise," maintains Moravia, "but only as a part of a work's structure. I am not a formalist and words interest me only insofar as they express a problem, become a problem." In *Agostino* he sees a poetic component that is perhaps stronger than in other works of his, possibly because of the partly autobiographical aspect of the protagonist. This in turn may account for the "elegance" of the prose even though his main concern was, as always, with the story itself—the drama of the boy's painful initiation into sex and the discovery of sin, his yearning to be a man, the conflict between his tender attachment to his mother and the surging hostility toward her that gradually draws him away. At the seashore Agostino joins a group of young hoodlums who congregate around a lecherous, six-fingered homosexual sailor. It is from them that he learns the basic facts of sex, theretofore totally excluded from his sheltered existence. The boy is denied, however, the physical experience of love; at the bordello he is turned away because of his age. Sex for him remains enveloped in a mist of turbid concupiscence and mystery that he knows he will be unable to penetrate until he grows older. "He was not a man yet," is his thought at the conclusion of the book—"and a long unhappy time had to pass before he could become one."

In 1948, six years after writing *Agostino*, Moravia published the sequel, *La disubbidienza* (Disobedience), another short novel of psychological analysis which ranks, with *Agostino*, among the best works of modern fiction on the theme of adolescence. (The two books were published together in English, under the joint title *Two Adolescents*, 1960.) "Disobedience" is the key word that illustrates the hostile attitude and behavior of the protagonist, Luca, toward persons and even objects in his environment. Luca, fifteen years old, is driven by a self-destructive urge, "a will of renunciation and resignation," Moravia calls it, that gradually turns him against his parents, his studies, his most precious personal possessions, and finally against his own life. He stops eating—supreme disobedience—and stoically awaits death. But his suicidal plan is thwarted by the arrival of a young woman, the governess of his three cousins who have been sent to Luca's home because their mother is ill. Luca first feels attracted to the governess because she is good-natured, unaffected, gay, and so completely different from his mother. Later, however, he understands that what really draws him to her is her sensuous femininity. The woman in turn is attracted to the boy; she flirts with him and invites him to her house on her day off. Luca burns with desire to make love to her but realizes that to do so would amount to reaccepting life. Still determined to pursue his nihilism to the end, he fails to keep the rendezvous. The following day his cousins leave, and the governess with them. He never sees her again. Before long his health begins to give way under the nervous strain of his determined disobedience, and for three months Luca remains seriously ill—he is often delirious. One day, as he recovers consciousness, his eyes focus upon the face of a woman, a stranger: the nurse. Much to his surprise, he feels a sudden impulse of "sympathy" for that face, and immediately after, for everything else in the room, including even his own face as he looks in a mirror. Thus Luca is cured. His new emotional disposition of "sympathy" toward life in general fosters the blossoming of an uncomplicated sexual relationship with the nurse. This initiation into sex, deftly narrated in some of the most effective pages of the book, is a refreshing and rewarding experience through which reality appears to the boy in a calm, friendly light. And the woman responsible for the change becomes for him a second mother, truer and more beneficent than his real one.

One moral to be drawn from Luca's story is that life is stronger than death, that the life instinct in man prevails over his death wish. This is also the underlying theme of *La romana* (1947, translated into English as *The Woman of Rome*), a work which preceded by a year *La disubbidienza* and with which Moravia returned to the long novel for the first time after *Le ambizioni sbagliate*.

La romana is scarcely one of Moravia's best works, despite the fact that it immediately became a best-seller and contributed substantially to his popularity, particularly abroad. It is diffuse, slow-moving, and it suffers especially from failure on the plane of credibility. Paralleling the structure of *Moll Flanders*, the book is the first-person account of the life of a prostitute and thief, Adriana. Although Moravia tries hard not to intellectualize the narration, only too often the discrepancy between the uneducated, peasant-class girl that the twenty-one-year-old Adriana is supposed to be and certain of her reflections and statements of a social, religious, and philosophical nature is simply too wide to be plausible. Yet, apart from its shortcomings, *La romana* marks a turning point in Moravia's development as a writer and announces two significant innovations—the introduction into his fiction of peasant- and working-class characters, and the use of first-person narrative—which will lead eventually to remarkable results in *I racconti romani* (1954), *La ciociara* (1957), and the brilliant "essay-novels" *La noia* (1960) and *L'attenzione* (1965).

Until the writing of *La romana*, Moravia for twenty years had been portraying characters and situations connected with the Italian bourgeoisie, primarily because it was the only social milieu he knew well. On the other hand, he admits freely to having always felt the utmost contempt for the vast majority of the middle and upper class in Italy—which he considered venal, corrupt, spineless, and above all "phony" (his word)—and to being progressively attracted to the lower classes, which alone appeared to him still basically genuine and "authentic." Gradually this attraction became a sort of myth, sexual as well as social, and one of its products was the creation of the persona of Adriana.

Moravia's first prolonged personal contact with simple, uneducated people occurred in 1943–44. Warned that the Gestapo was planning his arrest because of certain anti-Fascist articles he had written after the fall of Mussolini in July, 1943, the novelist left Rome with his wife and headed south, hoping to join the Allies. Unable to cross the lines, he took refuge in the isolated mountain hamlet of Fondi, halfway between Rome and Naples. There he spent nine months, sleeping in a stable and sharing the life of the local shepherds and peasants. After his return to Rome at the end of the war, he set out to write a novel centered upon his recent experiences; but probably because he felt they were still too close to him and he lacked the necessary perspective, he abandoned the project after having written some eighty pages. The writing of the novel, to be called *La ciociara* after the protagonist—a working-class woman from Ciociaria, the region south of Rome—was not resumed and completed for more than ten years. In the meantime Moravia started composing a short story about the relationship between two peasant women, a mother and her daughter who becomes a prostitute. But that short story kept growing, he recalls, and in barely four months it became a 500-page novel, the memoirs of Adriana, the "Woman of Rome."

The elaborate genesis of this first nonbourgeois character is significant because it illustrates how important and imperative —almost obsessive—the "myth" of the peasant and working class had become for Moravia. "In identifying myself with Adriana," he confesses, "I thought for a while that I had found the key to my own rapport with reality, with life." Certainly Adriana represents a triumph of the life force, and in this respect at least *La romana* is successful and convincing. Despite the suicide of Mino, the weak, irresolute man she loved, and despite her discovery that she is going to give birth to the child of Sonzogno, a murderer killed by the police, Adriana still finds it possible to face her future with calm confidence, indeed with hope. The book's final paragraph leaves no doubt in this respect:

I thought about Mino and then I thought about my child. I thought how he would be the child of a murderer and a prostitute; but any man in the world might happen to kill someone and any woman might sell herself for money; and what mattered most of all was that he should have an easy birth and grow up strong and healthy. I decided that if it was a boy I would call him Giacomo in memory of Mino. But if it was a girl, I would call her Letitia, because I wanted her to have what I had not had, a gay, happy life, and I was sure that, with the help of Mino's family, that was just what she would have.

Moravia's postwar writing is marked by two characteristics: its sheer volume and the shift from third- to first-person narration. This shift, far from being an external, technical factor, reflects a renewed attempt on his part to focus more sharply on the ever-present problem of rapport with reality. The use of the third person, he explains, implies the belief in the existence of an objective reality and in the possibility of portraying it objectively. But, as becomes increasingly evident, this belief can no longer be sustained with any degree of confidence: whenever a novelist writes "he thought," he faces a basic dilemma, because no one can know with certainty what anyone else is thinking. In other words, the mere fact of writing "he thought" strikes Moravia today as a meaningless convention; all a writer can say without deceiving himself and his reader is "*I* thought," thereby implicitly stating that reality can exist only—if at all—as the expression of the individual self. In a sense Moravia answers the question of the relationship between an author and his characters in much the same way that Flaubert did when he said "Madame Bovary c'est moi"; but in discarding the third person, Moravia goes one step beyond the French novelist.

The adoption of the first-person narrator, then, begun with *La romana* in 1947, became for Moravia a practice he would adhere to steadily up to the present day, with two exceptions: the previously mentioned *La disubbidienza* (1948), in which the third person was probably made imperative by the fact that Luca's story was a sequel to *Agostino;* and *Il conformista* (1951, translated into English as *The Conformist*), by unanimous consent (including Moravia's) his weakest novel, a contrived and unconvincing story about the political assassination of an anti-Fascist professor living in exile in France, and the personal drama of an insecure, tormented man, Marcello Clerici, who consents to organize the crime.

Before and after *Il conformista*, Moravia published two works on the theme of the marital relationship—a long story, *L'amore coniugale* (1949, translated into English as *Conjugal Love*), and a full-fledged novel, *Il disprezzo* (literally, "Contempt," translated into English as *A Ghost at Noon*, 1954). Like *La romana* they are first-person accounts, but there is no discrepancy here, as in Adriana's journal, between the narrator and the distinct literary flavor of the narration, since in both cases the husband, the narrating I, is an intellectual and a writer. *L'amore coniugale* is the study of a wife's adultery, of the events that lead up to it, and finally of the way in which the couple succeed in saving their marriage and preserving their "conjugal love." Though well structured and well written, it remains among Moravia's minor accomplishments. This cannot be said of *Il disprezzo*, which deals with the failure of a marriage and the range and depth of which single it out among Moravia's major achievements.

The novel raises and tries to answer a number of puzzling questions: why does a young wife, after two years of "perfect marriage," suddenly stop loving her husband? What can her reasons, her motivations be, since it appears that she is not in love with another man? Is her reason perhaps her husband's reluctant decision to give up temporarily his work as a playwright and seek an assignment as a movie scriptwriter for its higher financial rewards? Does the wife believe her husband is using her to persuade the producer to give him the job? But even if this were partly true, is it not clear to her that her husband is actually making a sacrifice to please her, accepting a distasteful compromise in order to give her the apartment she has always wanted? Riccardo Molteni, the husband, will never find a satisfactory answer to these questions, much as he may probe and implore Emilia. All he is able to learn from her is that she "despises" him—hence the book's Italian title. The title of the English version, *A Ghost at Noon*, reflects instead the more romantic aspect of the story. At the producer's villa in Capri, Riccardo tells Emilia that for her sake and to win back her love and respect he will not finish the movie script. Emilia icily replies that, no matter what he does, her contempt for him will persist. Soon afterwards she abandons him and leaves for Rome with the producer. But on the road their automobile collides at high speed with an ox-driven cart; Emilia dies instantly, her neck broken by the force of the impact. Meanwhile in Capri, Riccardo has not yet recovered from the stunning effect of his wife's last words. Despite the abyss of incomprehension that seems to divide them, he is still in love with her. And in his feverish agitation, intensified by the blazing sun of high noon, he experiences a hallucination. Emilia appears to him, asks his forgiveness for having misjudged him, assures him that she has never really despised him. When later Riccardo learns of his wife's death, he almost goes out of his mind. After the funeral in Rome he leaves the city —everything there now reminds him of her hostility and contempt—and returns to Capri. There he hopes that Emilia's ghost will again come to bring him comfort. He realizes, however, that he has reached the threshold of insanity, that he must find within himself, not in a dream, the answer to Emilia's inexplicable behavior. And it is then that, to gain some measure of objectivity, he starts to write out the story of their relationship.

Il disprezzo thus represents yet another chapter in Moravia's struggle to grasp and define an elusive reality, exemplified in this novel not only by the two antagonists, Riccardo and Emilia, but also by three different and conflicting interpretations of the legendary character of Ulysses. The script Riccardo first consents and later refuses to write is a cinematic version of the *Odyssey*. The producer wants to portray Ulysses as a conventional hero going from one spectacular adventure to the next. Riccardo, however, following the tradition established by Dante in the *Divine Comedy*, sees him as an idealist, ready to sacrifice his life for his beliefs. Finally, the German director, Rheingold, conceives of him as a man caught in the coils of a neurosis. Rheingold's reading of the *Odyssey* has brought him to some startling conclusions: first, Penelope despises Ulysses for his failure to react like a man, a husband, and a king to her suitors' indiscreet attentions; second, it is Penelope's contempt that prompts Ulysses' departure for the Trojan war; third, Ulysses, fully aware of his wife's feelings toward him, delays his return home as long as he can; fourth, in order to regain Penelope's esteem and love, he finally slays the suitors. Riccardo vehemently rejects Rheingold's interpretation although he sadly realizes that Emilia would in all probability agree with it. Should he kill the producer, as Ulysses did the suitors? But this, as well as all other questions raised in the course of the novel, is left unanswered. Riccardo may only hope to find some peace of mind through the act of writing his memoirs—a Pirandellian "novel within the novel" solution that Moravia later expanded in *L'attenzione*.

Il disprezzo, an immediate success, was made into a movie and received one of the major literary prizes, the Strega. In the same year (1954) Moravia collected in book form the sixty-odd "Racconti romani" (Roman Tales) that he had been publishing regularly in the *Corriere della sera*—rapid sketches of short, fixed length, often quite brilliant, written in the tradition of the famous nineteenth-century vernacular poet Giuseppe Gioacchino Belli, in which an anonymous Roman from the working class tells a story in the first person, usually a humorous anecdote with a satirical tang. But then, Moravia admits, for the second time in his career (the first had been after *Gli indifferenti*), he found himself at an impasse, drained of inspiration. For two years he tried vainly to complete a new novel based, in his own words, on a "rather curious idea"—the weird barter struck by two friends, one of whom offers his wife to the other if he will become a communist. Finally, in 1956, he reread the pages he had written and put aside more than ten years earlier, after returning home from his war experiences in the mountains, and in a very short time he succeeded in completing *La ciociara*. The book, published in 1957, was hailed as a major novel. The 1958 English translation, titled *Two Women*, was soon followed by a popular motion picture version.

The main strand along which the plot of *La ciociara* is woven is provided by the adventures of Cesira—a thirty-five-year-old widow who operates a grocery store in Rome's Trastevere—and of her teen-age daughter Rosetta. They flee the city in September, 1943, after the beginning of the Allied aerial bombardments, and try to reach Cesira's family's home in Vallecorsa, a mountain village on the road to Naples. But the village has already been evacuated and they have to settle down for nine months in a hut in nearby Sant'Eufemia with other refugees. After the liberation, as they prepare to return to Rome, Rosetta is raped in an abandoned church by a group of Moroccan soldiers attached to the French army. The savagery of that experience has the effect of transforming her from an innocent, shy, pious eighteen-year-old into a rabid nymphomaniac and prostitute. Only as the two women finally reach the outskirts of Rome does Rosetta seem to recover a sense of decency and compassion. Her latest lover, a black marketeer, is murdered before her eyes after Cesira has robbed him of his money. Mother and daughter are picked up by a truck; as they approach the end of their journey, Rosetta, until then silent and seemingly indifferent, suddenly starts to sing and to weep. Perhaps, as Cesira reflects in the concluding page of the book, they are being saved at the last moment by their common grief. Perhaps, she ponders hopefully, they are still basically the same guiltless human beings who had left Rome a year before, rather than the thief and the prostitute they had become through events they could neither foresee nor control.

But *La ciociara* is much more than the personal drama of Cesira and Rosetta. It is the story of a country at war, I would say the only major historical novel (with Manzoni's *Promessi sposi* a distant point of reference) written by an Italian to date with the second world conflict as background. Other fine books, of course, have come out of that matrix; one has only to mention the names of Calvino, Rimanelli, Pavese, Rigoni-Stern, Vittorini, Malaparte, Pirro, Ottieri, and Fenoglio. All these authors, however, have concerned themselves with special, single aspects or individual episodes of those years. *La ciociara* alone attempts to grasp and portray the collective, choral element of the war experience of the Italian people. In a sense the war is the real protagonist here, since around it revolve all the various characters that make up the large fresco

—the soldiers, the peasants, the refugees, the Nazis, the Fascists, the anti-Fascists, the racketeers. Three different planes are clearly distinguishable within the novel's structure, all in relation to the war. First, immediately before the war strikes the civilian population directly, life is almost happy despite the prevailing egoism and general indifference to the suffering of others. Then, as the war's full impact makes itself felt, there is the ever-present sense of physical danger, the anguish of not knowing what the future has in store, and the long, tormenting wait. This second phase has its historical counterpart in the interminable nine months during which the German and Allied forces faced each other across the Garigliano river between September, 1943, and June, 1944, and is typified by the minute, at times even exasperating description of the refugees' daily existence in Sant'Eufemia—a description of over 200 pages, more than half of the book. From this central portion of the novel emerges the only other main figure, Michele, perhaps the most "positive" character Moravia has created (and it is significant for an understanding of his development as an author that he should have called the youth by the same name he had given almost thirty years before to the anti-hero of *Gli indifferenti*). Michele, twenty-five, the only man of military age in Sant'Eufemia not in uniform because his father's influence and money have kept him from being drafted, is an intellectual and a rebel. Educated in Fascist and Catholic Italy, he is violently anti-Fascist and anti-clerical. The son of one of the wealthiest landowners of the area, he detests the family as an institution, attributing to it the origin of most of Italy's evils. He is especially outspoken against his father's and the other refugees' cupidity, avarice, and selfishness. He tells them that without knowing it they are really dead, that like Lazarus they will be able to come back to life only after becoming aware of their present state of moral and spiritual death. Of all the people in Sant'Eufemia, Michele befriends only Cesira and Rosetta, for despite their ignorance he recognizes in them a basic goodness and integrity. And when five retreating German soldiers start to drag Rosetta away as their hostage, he succeeds in persuading them to take him instead. The two women learn later that Michele was killed by his captors.

The third plane in the novel's structure carries us into the period following the arrival of the Allies and the liberation—days of short-lived exultation and hope after which things grow worse than before: the country in ruin, unemployment, and poverty; the sense of guilt for the Nazi and Fascist atrocities; renewed violence, insecurity, despair. To this section belong Rosetta's rape and consequent depravity and perversion, her lover's murder, and the theft of his money by Cesira. Thus, if one keeps in mind that *La ciociara*'s underlying theme is the war, one can also perceive that the figures of the two women have a symbolic meaning: they stand for Italy and the Italians. It is remarkable that Moravia should have achieved a choral effect of this kind with a novel narrated in the first person by a woman like Cesira. The obvious reason is that here he was able to overcome the dichotomy between narrating protagonist and author so often disturbing in *La romana*, and to attain, in the wake of the emotional impact of his personal experiences, a nearly perfect degree of identification with Cesira and her story. It was a success, however, that Moravia was well aware he could not duplicate, and with *La ciociara* his period of experimentation with narrating female characters as well as with people from the peasant and working classes comes virtually to an end. In his next two and, at the time of this writing, last novels, *La noia* and *L'attenzione*, he has concerned himself anew with the world closest to him, that of the Roman bourgeoisie scrutinized by a male intellectual.

La noia was published in 1960 after Moravia's engrossing report of his trip to Russia (*Un mese in URSS* [One Month in the USSR], 1958), after a theatrical version of *La mascherata* and an original play on the theme of patricide, *Beatrice Cenci* (both in the volume *Teatro* [Theatre], 1958), and after the appearance of a collection of 69 new "Roman Tales" (*Nuovi racconti romani*, 1959). Taking us back in many ways to *Gli indifferenti*, *La noia* is, with that first novel, probably Moravia's most important achievement. Moreover, its interest stems not only from the author's obvious literary mastery—notably his terse, lucid style and highly skillful characterization—but also from the fact that with it Moravia explicitly answers for the first time the question left open by all his works: in an age of insecure, estranged, and boredom-oppressed people, what hope does man—Moravia's contemporary man—have of being able to live at peace with himself, of coming to terms with and finding an acceptable *modus vivendi* within the reality of his time?

Both *La noia* and *L'attenzione* are what Moravia calls "essay-novels," each beginning with a "prologue" and ending with an "epilogue" in which the thesis, or theme, is respectively postulated and resolved. In the prologue of *La noia*, he defines through the protagonist-narrator, Dino, the concept of boredom which gives the book its title. Dino, a painter in his middle thirties who has been brought up and supported all his life by his wealthy mother, declares that he has always suffered from boredom, but that only in recent years has he been able to understand with any degree of clarity what boredom really is —"a kind of insufficiency or inadequacy or lack of reality." Boredom is, in other words, "incommunicability," an incapacity to establish and maintain a relationship with objects and other persons, an all-pervading feeling of "absurdity." Its principal aspect and most direct consequence is the "practical impossibility" of living happily with oneself, that is, as Dino observes wistfully, with the only person in the world one cannot forsake. Boredom has just caused Dino to decide to stop painting, a relatively new activity for him, but one through which he had hoped "to re-establish contact with reality." He is not, he warns, merely an unsuccessful painter conscious of his own failure:

Certainly I had failed, but not because I was unable to paint pictures that other people liked; it was rather because I felt that my pictures did not permit me to express myself, in other words to deceive myself into imagining that I had some contact with external things—in a word, they did not prevent me from being bored. Now the fundamental reason why I had started painting was to escape from boredom. If I went on being bored, why go on painting?

With a knife Dino slashes his last painting and puts on the easel in its place a blank canvas, to which he later affixes his name as the only work he feels he can sign (hence the title chosen for *La noia*'s English version: *The Empty Canvas*). Some time later, returning to his studio after a visit to his mother's luxurious villa on the Via Appia, he meets a young girl of seventeen, Cecilia, the former model and mistress of another painter, a certain Balestrieri. Balestrieri, an older man with a reputation for eroticism, had died the day before of a heart attack. Irresistibly and although unable to account for his compulsive curiosity, Dino starts questioning Cecilia about her relationship with the painter. The girl answers every question readily, with polite patience, but somehow always evasively, or so at least Dino feels at the end of the conversation. "Yes," he confesses to himself, "I had learned many things, but my lack of satisfaction made it clear that the thing which really mattered to me had escaped me." Thus from that first encounter Cecilia appears to Dino to be endowed with a mysterious power which he cannot define and much less control—a power which arouses in him, against his will, "a disconcerting sense of fascinated attraction." Dino and Cecilia become lovers that same day and for the next two months meet with increasing frequency, until the old, unmistakable feeling of boredom assails Dino once more:

By this time I realized that I was beginning to be bored with Cecilia, to find myself once more in the state of isolation and detachment in which I had been just before I met her. . . . In reality it was not that Cecilia was boring, it was I who was bored, even though I knew in my heart that I might very well not be bored if, by some miracle, I could succeed in making my relationship with her more real. On the contrary, however, I felt it growing weaker and emptier every day.

Finally Dino decides to end his affair with Cecilia. He buys an expensive alligator handbag as a parting gift, planning to give it to her at her next visit. But Cecilia, until then so punctual and dependable, this time fails to keep the rendezvous. This unforeseen, apparently trivial development completely upsets Dino and marks for him the beginning of a real drama of truly ontological proportions. Until then he had practically forced himself to believe that Cecilia was "nothing" to him, or little more than just another "object." Now, however, he has to admit that she is "something," even though what that something is completely escapes him. Dino would still wish to get rid of Cecilia, but of the Cecilia who loves him, not of the Cecilia who shows her indifference by missing the rendezvous. And this, as he painstakingly explains to himself, "was not a case of that special, perverse kind of love which makes us love someone who does not love us and dislike anyone who does love us; it was because the Cecilia who loved me had proved boring, and therefore unreal, whereas the Cecilia who did not love me seemed, on the contrary, by the very fact of not loving me, to acquire a steadily increasing semblance of reality in my eyes."

Dino's reflection illumines the particular meanings that Moravia attributes to such terms as "boring," "unreal," "reality"—key words in the realm of *La noia*. "Boring" is synonymous with "unreal"—and we have already seen that boredom is caused by "incommunicability," by the interruption of the rapport between self and reality. This interruption occurs, as Moravia notes in another central passage, when we become aware that we have exhausted all rapport with an object, when no further comprehension or, as it were, possession of the object appears likely or possible. Dino destroys his last painting once it becomes totally *unreal* to him, that is, when, as he phrases it, like a tumbler or any other too familiar object it "withers away and loses its vitality . . . or, in other words, reveals itself to me as something foreign, something with which I have no relationship . . . an absurd object." Conversely, "reality" is what is *not* boring because it still withholds a part unknown, something that is yet to be probed, understood, conquered, albeit at the price of suffering. This last consideration makes Dino hope that Cecilia still loves him and that consequently he need not alter his decision to end their liaison: "because the idea that she had ceased to bore me, in other words that she was becoming real, filled me, fundamentally, with a kind of fear, as though I were confronting a trial that I did not feel able to face."

But Cecilia *is* real—indeed, as Dino explicitly admits some time later, she is reality itself. She is real and desirable precisely because she is "something problematic and elusive," the more so when Dino learns that she lies to him. Cecilia, the strange woman-child whose nature and impulses seem to be regulated solely by her voracious sexuality, is an "object" which Dino cannot truly "possess." Despite the "masculine illusion which looks upon physical possession as the only true possession," he has to confess that "the more I had her the less I possessed her," for "Cecilia's body was not Cecilia, and what Cecilia was, I could not find out." At one point, toward the end of the novel, he is drawn to the following bitter conclusion: "In our relationship it was she, in reality, who possessed me, and I who was possessed, although nature, for her own ends, deceived both Cecilia and me into thinking the opposite."

The day after Cecilia's failure to come to his studio, Dino accidentally discovers that she has a second lover, an actor named Luciani. While the grief he experiences at this discovery reinforces his determination to break with her, he realizes that he is unable to carry out his decision so long as Cecilia's behavior causes him to suffer. He also understands that with Cecilia his only alternatives are to be bored or to suffer. While he was bored he wanted to leave her; now that he is suffering, obviously the only way to leave her is to become bored again. But Cecilia in the end drives him to despair, not to boredom. And from the moment Dino decides to cast her off the novel becomes paradoxically the story of an unsuccessful attempt at self-induced *noia*.

As a first step, Dino forces Cecilia to confess her betrayal with Luciani, which she does very matter-of-factly but without appearing, as Dino had hoped, "discredited and reduced to nothingness" in his eyes. Then he tries to convince himself that there is no mystery or anything unusual about her, that she is simply venal and motivated by greed. Cecilia, however, is personally not interested in money: whatever she receives from Dino she gives to Luciani, who is temporarily without work and whom she now sees constantly, even on the days when she meets Dino. Dino, tormented by the thought that Luciani might have succeeded in truly "possessing" Cecilia and solely by means of the sexual act, which had proved so insufficient in his case, in desperation concludes that "the only way to set [himself] free from Cecilia—that is, possess her and consequently become bored with her—was to marry her." But Cecilia does not want to marry him; she is planning instead to go to the island of Ponza for a vacation with Luciani. And when Dino, in a magnificent Rabelaisian scene, literally covers her naked body from head to foot with banknotes and offers her all the money she wants if she will only remain with him, Cecilia modestly asks for a small loan to finance her trip with the actor. Enraged, Dino is about to strangle her, but is stopped by the thought that a dead Cecilia would elude him forever. Cecilia leaves for Ponza. Dino, half insane with frustration, drives his automobile headlong into a tree. But he does not die. He regains consciousness in a hospital bed, immobilized in a plaster cast with his head turned toward the window.

Outside that window, in full view, is a great cedar of Lebanon. Day after day Dino gazes at it until gradually—in a scene that brings to mind at the same time Luca's awakening in the nurse's presence in *La disubbidienza*, and the finale in Pirandello's novel *One, No-One, One-Hundred-Thousand*—he realizes that he is accepting the tree's "reality" as that of an object removed from him, with which he has no rapport but which nonetheless is impossible to ignore. Somehow the tree's autonomy, the fact of its being different and separate from him, fills Dino with "infinite pleasure." Moreover, he soon comes to feel that he can extend this pleasure to include any other "object"—and therefore also Cecilia. And so, the thought of her in Ponza, contented with her lover, now makes him "happy." In short, he no longer desires to "possess" her but simply wishes to watch her live her life, to "contemplate" her just as he contemplates the tree out of the window. "This contemplation," he reflects, "would never come to an end for the simple reason that I did not wish it to come to an end, that is, I did not wish the tree, or Cecilia, or any other object outside myself, to become boring to me and consequently to cease to exist. . . . Once I was well, I would go back to the studio and try to start painting again."

Thus with *La noia*, Moravia breaks the vicious circle of despair and self-destruction in which some of his most typical characters are imprisoned, and in his own way tries to bring to a solution that psychological crisis of modern man's rapport with reality around which, as Moravia himself stated, his entire work revolves. Dino, unable to face reality, attempts suicide: it is the "plunge to the bottom of the abyss" of which Baudelaire spoke. He is saved, one might say, because the abyss somehow rejects him. But his salvation—although he does not realize it until after his narrow escape from death, and possibly not quite fully even then—began with his encounter with Cecilia, who by her elusiveness made it impossible for him to "possess" her and thus to relapse into boredom. And so, Moravia seems to say, if there is hope for man, it lies in the discovering of an "object" which cannot be fully possessed, which refuses to yield the key to its secret, its mystery, its individuality, but can be accepted only as it is, in its unique diversity.

This is of course a conclusion with a definitely mystical, even religious flavor, surprising perhaps from an author like Moravia. Nevertheless it is unmistakably what he had in mind. In 1961, one year after *La noia*'s enormous and unprecedented success (it received the Viareggio Prize and quickly sold 250,000 copies in Italy alone), Moravia declared in an interview: "With Dino, for the first time I felt I could conclude a novel by explicitly pointing to a moral: life can be contemplation, it does not have to be action, as Michele thought in *Gli indifferenti*. I do not pretend this to be the only admissible moral, but it is the only one I personally have arrived at, at the age of fifty-three." Later, in another statement released the same year, made in response to the reservations of some critics who charged that the conclusion of *La noia* appears forced and unconvincing, he carried his reflections further. Having built his novel, he said, around the problem of possession of reality, he had become convinced that he owed it to himself, and to his readers, to tell how his protagonist had achieved this possession. "Not that I had decided to explain it for some whimsical motive," he insisted, "but because I had been able to see in my own life that possession can be attained perhaps only . . . through contemplation of the object. In *La noia* this contemplation is twofold: its first aspect is, obviously, aesthetic; the second is religious and mystical, because only through contemplation does one attain perfect objectiveness."

The theme of contemplation is underscored once again—but from a different angle, as we shall see—in Moravia's latest novel, *L'attenzione* (Attention, 1965). In this captivatingly intricate book a journalist, Francesco Merighi, first destroys a novel he had written (just as Dino did his last painting) and decides instead to keep a diary, planning to extract a novel from it afterwards. But at the end he discovers that the diary is the very novel he had wanted to write in the first place—a novel, however, whose real protagonist turns out to be not the narrator but the novel itself. In other words, structurally speaking, *L'attenzione* is a "novel's novel," not unlike Pirandello's play-within-a-play, *Six Characters in Search of an Author*. From this point of view one can understand why *L'attenzione*'s English translation is entitled *The Lie*, for the book deals undeniably also with ambiguity and even duplicity. One must keep in mind, on the other hand, that the novel's emphasis is not on deception but on truth: Francesco's diary is literally a means by which he dedicates his "attention" to the discovery of the truth. He regards his diary-novel less as a literary genre than as a way of understanding his relationship with reality, indeed as his "conscience." "In the diary," he says, "I interpret reality, I adapt it, I reconstruct it, I integrate it, I complete it . . . [but] I am not inventing anything. . . . The truth, perceived by intuition and reconstructed, is not fundamentally altered." And in an essay entitled "The Novel's Novel: Notes for *L'attenzione*," published shortly after the work had appeared, Moravia includes a statement that reads like a rejoinder to Francesco's observations: "Of course the novelist is a liar," he declares, "but the purpose of a novel's novel is precisely to reveal the truth that hides behind the lies."

In the novel that he destroys, Francesco had told the story of his love for a dressmaker, Cora Mancini, from their first meeting to the day of their marriage. Soon after the wedding, however, he realizes that he is no longer in love with Cora and that he wishes to have as little as possible to do with her and her twenty-year-old daughter, Baba, who had been born during the war of a liaison with a German soldier. At the same time he becomes convinced to his horror that his novel sounds hopelessly false, "unauthentic" (this and its opposite, "authentic," are key words throughout), despite the fact that it is based entirely on actual events and actual characters. In desperation he tears up the manuscript and throws the scraps of paper out of the window.

For the next ten years Francesco manages to spend most of

his time on journalistic assignments away from home. He still lives with Cora and Baba but he sees them only sporadically, between trips. These are for him, Francesco notes, years of almost total estrangement, of "disattenzione" ("inattention"), in the sense that he is able to keep his mind off his family, particularly Cora. One thing only remains unchanged in his life: his ambition to write a novel. For years during his professional travels he ponders about the manuscript he had written and destroyed. Why had it turned out to be so "unauthentic"? Because, he concludes, it was based on facts which were narrated as "actions":

Now here lay the truth of the matter; the artificiality of the novel derived from the action that took place within it. I had in fact verified that in the reality of life it was not possible, for me at any rate, to act in a genuine manner. In consequence—like a subtle poison which has become blended with the soil and which passes through the roots of a tree into its most intimate fibers—artificiality had penetrated, from the things I had tried to depict, into the very words I had used to depict them.

Francesco's predicament reminds us in many ways of Dino's in *La noia*. What the former calls, in the Italian original, "inautenticità ("lack of authenticity," and therefore, as the English text has it, "artificiality") is patently akin to Dino's "boredom." What then, asks Francesco, is an "authentic" novel? His answer is: a novel that excludes every kind of "dramatic action," "a novel without a story, without a series of events, without drama, a novel in which nothing happens." And "what is the opposite of dramatic action? The opposite of dramatic action is the ordinary run of things, the routine, as they say, of everyday life." Thus Francesco resolves to keep a diary during one of his visits home between journeys:

A diary of two months of my life. Then from this diary I would extract the novel—that is, an objective narrative in the third person and the past definite tense. After the novel of artificiality, based on action, it would be the novel of the genuine, based on everyday life.

In the process of writing the diary, indeed *through* the diary itself used as a mirror for his daily thoughts, Francesco is able to reconstruct the story of his involvement with Cora, both before and after their marriage. In the central, or "diary," part of the novel (the other two parts are, as in *La noia*, the "prologue" and the "epilogue"), we learn that Cora has become a procuress, that she has even tried to involve Baba in her illicit traffic, and, most important, that Francesco and Baba have fallen in love.

The main interest of *L'attenzione*, as well as its message, hinges upon this "incestuous" attraction between stepfather and stepdaughter, together with its implications and perils. Moravia, of course, is not concerned with morality in a conventional sense but with the "authenticity" or, if one likes, the quality of love. Francesco's love for Cora had proved "unauthentic" and had led to estrangement and boredom because it was acted upon and consummated. To preserve the "authenticity" of his love for Baba, Francesco now realizes that the only relationship they can have is the one that exists between an author and his characters—a rapport of "contemplation," as he explains to the girl.

This is because the love that I feel for you in real life is merely a mode of action, and there can be no genuineness in action, whereas the love which will allow me to represent you in my novel begins and ends in contemplation and does not become soiled with action, with the dream of action, or with the renunciation of action. I love you with this kind of love, and for that reason I am grateful to you as one ought to be grateful to someone who has aroused in one a rare, difficult, precious feeling.

To act, then, is by Moravia's definition unauthentic, for authenticity can exist only *before* one acts. Our world, says

Moravia in one of the most striking images in the novel, was authentic before God created it. To maintain oneself, as it were, in a state of authenticity, one must pay "attention" to avoid consuming and degrading by actions what is authentic in man —that is, thought in all its manifestations, from fantasies and dreams to contemplation. Thought-not-translated-into-action is one thing in cosmic creation that is not false: the world—the idea of the world—was genuine and pure in God's mind. And so the only authentic novel is the "diary" in its most spontaneous and direct form, in its closest, most faithful coincidence with thought—even, or rather all the more so, when it records alongside with actual events those that are imagined or invented, as is often the case with Francesco's diary in *L'attenzione*.

There is of coure an obvious and inescapable contradiction in all this. Even a "diary," once written, let alone published and sold commercially, is necessarily an act, and therefore unauthentic. Absolute authenticity in this respect is impossible, but the concept nevertheless subsists meaningfully as an ideal, a myth. The same is true for the ideal of "absolute silence" in poetry: the poet may pursue it in his own mind as the ultimate goal, but must know he will never be able to share it with others, as art. What we are witnessing in *L'attenzione* is therefore a novelist's search for a compromise between the unattainable absolute—wordless contemplation—and the urge to speak and be heard. The "diary" is described as the purest narrative because it is essentially an anti-novel, a form capable in the highest possible degree of preserving that authenticity of thought which is lost, according to Moravia, in traditional novels, all of which are based on "action."

Certainly with *La noia* and *L'attenzione* Moravia has reached an extreme limit in his development as a novelist, and he is well aware of it. "*L'attenzione*," he admits, "is a turning point in my career, a self-critique of my own work. In a way," he adds, "it is something of a catastrophe for me as a novelist. I know now there are certain things I can no longer do; I do not think I could write another realistic novel, for example. The theatre, I believe, is today the only medium left to me for expressing my ideas."

In addition to *La noia* and *L'attenzione*, Moravia has published during the last decade two thought-provoking journals, one of a trip to India (*Un'idea dell'India* [An Idea of India], 1962), the other of a visit to Communist China during the Red Guards' cultural revolution (*La rivoluzione culturale in Cina*, 1967, translated into English as *The Red Book and the Great Wall*, 1968); a rich selection of his own critical essays, indispensable for anyone who wants to follow his intellectual development (*L'uomo come fine*, 1964, translated as *Man as an End*, 1966); two collections of short stories (*L'automa*, 1963, translated as *The Fetish*, 1965; *Una cosa è una cosa*, 1967, translated as *Command, and I Will Obey You*, 1969); and three plays, *Il mondo è quello che è* (The World Is What It Is, 1966), a witty experiment in "language therapy" suggested by Wittgenstein's philosophy; *Il dio Kurt* (The God Kurt, 1968), a grim reenactment of the Oedipus tragedy in a Nazi concentration camp; and *La vita è gioco* (Life Is Play, 1969), which asserts that life should be treated as a game since it cannot be lived "logically"—and which ends with the death of all the major characters. While these works contribute to Moravia's solid reputation in contemporary literature, where *Gli indifferenti*, *Agostino*, *La disubbidienza*, *Il disprezzo*, *La ciociara*, *La noia*, and *L'attenzione* have already secured him a distinguished place, they attest especially to his continued militancy as a creative writer. Now in his early sixties, Moravia is still to be considered an author "in progress," endowed with an undaunted will for experimentation and self-renewal. At this writing (1969), while pursuing his interest in the theatre, he is also working on a new novel, which he hopes will be "free of schemas and constrictions, with the maximum of lyricism, of lyric liberty." Only recently he confided: "I write a novel in order to know why I write a novel. We live for continual discovery."

SELECTED BIBLIOGRAPHY

NOTE: *For extensive bibliographies of Moravia see the appendixes of the monographic studies by O. del Buono, A. Limentani, F. Longobardi, E. Sanguineti, and I. Scaramucci listed below. Moravia's complete works are published in Italy by Bompiani, in England by Secker & Warburg, and in the United States by Farrar, Straus & Giroux. Unless otherwise specified, Moravia's statements quoted in the text appear in one of the publications listed below, or were made during a hitherto unpublished, four-hour interview recorded on tape at the Italian Institute of Culture in New York on May 19–20, 1968.*

Principal Works of Alberto Moravia

Gli indifferenti, 1929. (The Time of Indifference, 1953.)
Le ambizioni sbagliate, 1935. (The Wheel of Fortune, 1937. Mistaken Ambitions, 1965.)
La mascherata, 1941. (The Fancy Dress Party, 1952.)
L'epidemia: Racconti surrealistici e satirici, 1944.
Agostino, 1944. (Two Adolescents, 1960.)
La romana, 1947. (The Woman of Rome, 1949.)
La disubbidienza, 1948. (Two Adolescents, 1960.)
L'amore coniugale e altri racconti, 1949. (Conjugal Love, 1951.)
Il conformista, 1951. (The Conformist, 1952.)
Racconti, 1952. (A selection from this book and from L'amore coniugale e altri racconti appeared in Bitter Honeymoon and Other Stories, 1954; a further selection appeared in The Wayward Wife and Other Stories, 1960.)
Il disprezzo, 1954. (A Ghost at Noon, 1955.)
Racconti romani, 1954. (Roman Tales, 1956.)
La ciociara, 1957. (Two Women, 1958.)
"Frammento di autobiografia," *Palatina*, October–December, 1958, pp. 3–6.
La noia, 1960. (The Empty Canvas, 1961.)
"Dialogo sul romanzo," *Quaderni milanesi*, No. 2 (1961), pp. 9–20.
"Dialogo, 21 aprile 1961," in Scrittori su nastro, II, 71–78. Milan, 1965.
L'uomo come fine e altri saggi, 1964. (Man as an End, 1965.)
L'attenzione, 1965. (The Lie, 1966.)

Critical Works and Commentary

Baldanza, Frank. "Mature Moravia," *Contemporary Literature*, IX, No. 4 (Autumn, 1968), 506–21.

Cowley, Malcolm. Writers at Work: The *Paris Review* Interviews, pp. 209–30. New York, 1959.

Cimmino, N. F. Lettura di Moravia. Rome, 1966.

Dego, Giuliano. Moravia. Edinburgh and London, 1966.

Del Buono, Oreste. Moravia. Milan, 1962.

De Michelis, Eurialo. Introduzione a Moravia. Florence, 1954.

Fernandez, Dominique. "Essai sur Alberto Moravia," in Le roman italien et la crise de la conscience moderne, pp. 9–138. Paris, 1958.

Heiney, Donald. "Alberto Moravia," in Three Italian Novelists, pp. 1–82. Ann Arbor, 1968.

Lewis, R. W. B. "Alberto Moravia: Eros and Existence," in The Picaresque Saint, pp. 36–56. Philadelphia and New York, 1961.

Limentani, Alberto. Alberto Moravia tra esistenza e realtà. Venice, 1962.

Longobardi, Fulvio. Moravia. Florence, 1969.

Pacifici, Sergio. "Alberto Moravia," in A Guide to Contemporary Italian Literature, pp. 29–56. New York, Meridian Books, 1962.

Rebay, Luciano. "Moravia: storia e strascichi di uno 'pseudonimo,'" *Forum Italicum*, IV, No. 1 (March, 1970), 16–22.

Sanguineti, Edoardo. Alberto Moravia. Milan, 1962.

Scaramucci, Ines. "Alberto Moravia," in I contemporanei, II, 1455–88. Milan, 1963.